First Workshop on Curation and Applications of Parallel and Comparable Corpora (Cupral 2017)

Taipei, Taiwan
27 November 2017

ISBN: 978-1-5108-5298-3

Printed from e-media with permission by:

Curran Associates, Inc.
57 Morehouse Lane
Red Hook, NY 12571

proceedings.com

Some format issues inherent in the e-media version may also appear in this print version.

Printed by Curran Associates, Inc. (2017)

Association for Computational Linguistics
209 N. Eighth Street
Stroudsburg, Pennsylvania 18360

Phone: 1-570-476-8006
Fax: 1-570-476-0860

acl@aclweb.org

Additional copies of this publication are available from:

Curran Associates, Inc.
57 Morehouse Lane
Red Hook, NY 12571 USA
Phone: 845-758-0400
Fax: 845-758-2633
Email: curran@proceedings.com
Web: www.proceedings.com

Cupral 2017

The First Workshop on Curation and Applications of Parallel and Comparable Corpora

Proceedings of the Workshop

November 27, 2017
Taipei, Taiwan

Introduction

The First Workshop on Curation and Applications of Parallel and Comparable Corpora (Cupral 2017) took place on Monday, November 27, 2017 in Taipei, Taiwan, immediately preceding the International Conference on Natural Language Processing (IJCNLP 2017).

The focus of our workshop was to explore the multifarious aspects of effective document alignment in multimodal and multilingual context. Most businesses operating across international borders understand the value of localization. In order to make a connection they have to be able to speak the language of their customers. Websites, marketing materials, news and other high-impact elements should all be thoroughly localized, which can mean a combination of computer vision (CV) and text processing in many target languages.

Clearly, techniques of Natural Language Processing (NLP) and Information Retrieval (IR) can be incredibly useful and further their combination with CV can potentially improve state-of-the-art document alignment research. Additionally, the aligned multimodal documents can be seamlessly used to improve the quality of predictive analytics on multi-modal data involving both text and images, e.g. the associated images of news articles may be utilized to help improve the ranks of these articles in a search engine or to translate the article better in a different language.

The workshop aimed to provide a forum for researchers working on related fields to present their results and insights. Our goal was to bring together researchers from diverse fields, such as CV, IR and NLP, who can potentially contribute to improving the quality of multimodal document alignment and its utilization in research and industrial data analytics tasks. The workshop was a starting point for an international platform dedicated to new method and techniques on aligning multimodal and multilingual documents, and exploring the use of such technology in NLP or IR.

Manoj Kumar Chinnakotla from Microsoft gave the invited on "Leveraging Parallel and Comparable Corpora for Multilingual NLP".

We would like to thank the members of the Program Committee for their timely reviews. We also would like to thank the participants of the workshop for the interesting discussions around our Cupal 2017 topics.

Haithem Afli & Chao-Hong Liu

Organizers:

Haithem Afli, ADAPT Centre, Dublin City University
Chao-Hong Liu, ADAPT Centre, Dublin City University

Program Committee:

Debasis Ganguly, Dublin Research Lab, IBM Ireland
Longyue Wang, Dublin City University
Alberto Poncelas, Dublin City University
Iacer Calixto, ADAPT Centre, Dublin City University

Additional Reviewers:

Walid Aransa, LIUM, Le Mans University
Pintu Lohar, Dublin City University

Invited Speaker:

Manoj Kumar Chinnakotla, Microsoft, India

Table of Contents

Workshop Program

Monday, November 27, 2017

08:00–09:10 *Registration*

09:15–9:30 *Opening Remarks*

09:30–10:30 ***Keynote Talk by Manoj Kumar Chinnakotla (Microsoft) on "Leveraging Parallel and Comparable Corpora for Multilingual NLP"***

10:30–11:00 *Coffee Break*

Presentations Session

11:00–11:30 *Building a Better Bitext for Structurally Different Languages through Self-training*
Jungyeul Park, Loic Dugast, Jeen-Pyo Hong, Chang-Uk Shin and Jeong-Won Cha

11:30–12:00 *MultiNews: A Web collection of an Aligned Multimodal and Multilingual Corpus*
Haithem Afli, Pintu Lohar and Andy Way

12:00–12:30 *Learning Phrase Embeddings from Paraphrases with GRUs*
zhihao zhou, Lifu Huang and Heng Ji

12:30–12:45 *Closing Session*

Building a Better Bitext for Structurally Different Languages Through Self-training

Jungyeul Park* **Loïc Dugast†** **Jeen-Pyo Hong‡** **Chang-Uk Shin§** **Jeong-Won Cha§**
*Department of Linguistics. University of Arizona. Tucson, AZ 85721
†Academy of African Language and Science, University of South Africa, South Africa
‡NAVER Corporation, Republic of Korea
§Department of Computer Engineering, Changwon National University. Republic of Korea
`http://air.changwon.ac.kr`

Abstract

We propose a novel method to bootstrap the construction of parallel corpora for new pairs of structurally different languages. We do so by combining the use of a pivot language and self-training. A pivot language enables the use of existing translation models to bootstrap the alignment and a self-training procedure enables to achieve better alignment, both at the document and sentence level. We also propose several evaluation methods for the resulting alignment.

1 Introduction

A parallel corpus is a pair of texts written in different languages which are translation of each other. Since multilingual publication has become more widespread, there is an increasing amount of such parallel data available. Those are valuable resources for linguistic research and natural language processing applications, such as machine translation. It is also valuable when building cross-lingual information retrieval software. Finding the corresponding documents between two languages is a required step to build a parallel corpus, before more fine-grained alignments (paragraphs and sentences) can be calculated. In some scenarios, multilingual data with identical or considerably similar texts can be found with more than two languages involved. We ask whether a language can help as a pivot when aligning corpora and whether self-training may bring additional improvement of the alignment quality. We see further that both questions can be answered positively.

We propose a novel method to efficiently build better parallel corpora through the combination of pivot language and self-training. This method is especially targeted at aligning structurally different languages. We present a topic-based document alignment algorithm and a length and lexicon-based sentence alignment algorithm. Instead of directly aligning languages with widely different structures and even different writing systems, we make use of a pivot language and translate the other language into this pivot language before performing alignment. Translation can be done with a statistical translation model if previous existing parallel data exist. In our case, we perform a joint alignment and training of a translation model for the Korean-English language pair. We use English as a pivot language. Therefore, Korean sentences are translated into English before getting aligned. That is, we align English and English-translated Korean instead of directly aligning English and Korean. In the end, alignments are restored in the original languages to build a parallel corpus. We also employ a self-trained translation model in which the statistical translation model is reinforced by the newly aligned data.

The contribution of this work is mainly as follows: (1) We use a pivot language to align two languages with different writing systems. (2) We propose a self-training method to be able to produce better parallel corpora. (3) We describe the basic preprocessing scheme for Korean to be able to improve the statistical machine translation results. (4) We also propose several experiments for aligned parallel corpora by providing a standard

* Most work has been done when J. Park was at the University of Arizona and L. Dugast was at the University of South Africa. Current J. Park's affiliation is CONJECTO, Rennes, France and L. Dugast's affiliation is TextMaster, Paris, France.

Proceedings of the Workshop on Curation and Applications of Parallel and Comparable Corpora, pages 1–10,
Taipei, Taiwan, November 27–December 1, 2017. ©2017 AFNLP

evaluation data set for Korean. We hope that the present work will pave the way for further development of machine translation for Korean.

2 Case Study for Crawling Parallel Documents from the Web

When we try to build a good parallel corpus by crawling bilingual (or multilingual) documents from the Web, we may encounter unexpected difficulties. In this section, we show a case study to point out these difficulties in building a parallel corpus for Korean using bilingual documents crawled from the Web. We obtain the bilingual data from the KOREANA website, a quarterly journal published on-line.[1] It offers information on Korean culture, originally written in Korean, along with their translations into several languages. For our small experiments in this case study, we work on web pages written in Korean and their translations into English. We first align documents then sentences. We crawl and prepare 348 Korean and 381 English documents of the time-span (2005-2014). Sentences in (1-4) extracted from a document of the KOREANA site, show the example results of alignment by our proposed method (alignment through translation and self-training) as described in §3.

After aligning documents and sentences, results on Korean-English machine translation do not improve when using the newly produced aligned corpus. Actually, even though they present relatively *good* quality of document and sentence alignments, we notice that all English sentences do not exactly correspond to Korean sentences, but are rather loose translation of them or even involve substantial rewriting. Mismatches of the words in the aligned sentences are represented in gray. We also estimate their correctness of translation by a ratio which we simply calculate based on the number of correctly translated words into English and the number of correctly translated words from Korean as follows:

$$\text{Correctness of translation} = \frac{\text{\# of correctly translated words}}{\text{Total \# of words}} \tag{1}$$

where # are the number of words in Korean and English. Such mismatches in the aligned corpus will generate in bad quality of the translation model. We estimate that over half of English sentences are not exactly translated from Korean.

[1] http://www.koreana.or.kr

description	notation
KO corpus	C_k
EN translated KO corpus	$C^i_{k'}$
EN corpus	C_e
Bilingual KO-EN	BC^i_{KOEN}
KOEN MT system	$MT(\sum_i BC^i_{\text{KOEN}})$

Table 1: Notations for the Bilingual Setting

Therefore, even though we can align correctly such a corpus at the sentence level, we may not obtain good quality of the translation model. Actually, many sites which provide bilingual (or multilingual) language services, especially translated from Korean into other language, show similar characteristics. We consider that they are rather comparable corpora and it would be difficult to expect good quality of sentence-aligned data from these sites. Working on comparable corpora is beyond the scope of this paper.

3 Proposed Method

Notations for this self-training setting are described in Table 1.

3.1 Document alignment

For the document alignment task, we make the hypothesis that some topics are similar or even identical between the original and its translations. We can therefore make use of a topic model to find the similarity between two documents. Probabilistic topic models enable to discover the thematic structure of a large collection of documents. It provides a latent topic representation of the corpus. Latent Dirichlet Allocation (LDA) is one of the most used type of topic models (Blei et al., 2003). In LDA, a document may be viewed as a mixture of topics and represented as a vector. This enables the comparison of document topics in a vector space.

The cosine similarity measure is applied to two latent vectors of documents in different languages. Let $similarity(d_{L_1}, d_{L_2})$ the cosine similarity between two documents in two different languages L_1 and L_2. This cosine similarity is calculated as follows:

$$similarity(d_{L_1}, d_{L_2}) = \frac{V_{d_{L_1}} \cdot V_{d_{L_2}}}{\|V_{d_{L_1}}\| \|V_{d_{L_2}}\|} \tag{2}$$

where two word vectors of $V_{d_{L_1}}$ and $V_{d_{L_2}}$ are from two documents in L_1 and L_2 languages. Instead of

(1) a. 그러나 경복궁에는 조선 창업의 뜻이 담겨 있으며, 500여 년 동안 조선을 상징하는 장소로 인식되었다.

b. Still, Gyeongbokgung does embody the spirit of the Joseon founders and for some 500 years has stood as an enduring symbol of the Joseon dynasty. (97.01%)

(2) a. 그러한 경복궁에 일본 식민지 통치를 위한 중추 기관인 조선총독부 신청사를 건설한 것은 지독히도 폭력적인 방법이었다.

b. Since Korea's liberation in 1945, there had been calls for the removal of the government general's building, which served as a painful reminder of Japan's colonial rule. (64.47%)

(3) a. 1990년대 조선총독부 건물을 헐어내고 경복궁을 복원하기 시작한 것은 사실 매우 논란의 여지가 있는 작업이다.

b. But upon the demolition of this building in the early 1990s, which enabled the Gyeongbokgung restoration project to get underway, even this was not free of its own controversy. (63.51%)

(4) a. 그러나 이러한 기억 투쟁이 식민지 시기를 떨쳐내고자 하는 사회적 요구에 의한 것이라는 점도 부인할 수는 없다.

b. In any case, no one can dispute the value of restoring Gyeongbokgung to its former glory and magnificence. (18.75%)

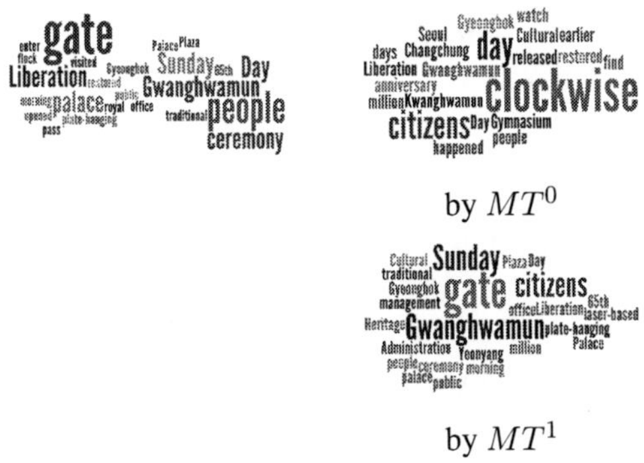

by MT^0

by MT^1

(a) English (b) Translated Korean

Figure 1: Examples of topic models in English and translated English from Korean

using all words in the document, we build these vectors from the topic models described above. Given a document in Korean and English, we translate them into English using the trained statistical translation models. We know that original Korean and English topic models do not directly share their elements in a vector space. However, translated Korean and English data by MT^0 show increasingly similar topic models and they become visibly related to each other. This situation improved further after self-training by MT^1 (See Figure 1). Measuring such similarity is hardly possible without using a pivot language or translated resources (Wu and Wang, 2007, 2009).[2]

3.2 Sentence alignment

Sentence alignment has been well-studied in the early 1990s (Brown et al., 1991; Chen, 1993; Gale and Church, 1993; Kay and Roscheisen, 1993). However, development of machine translation research demands increasing volumes of parallel data. This situation has led to the reinvestigation of sentence alignment such as in Moore (2002) and Varga et al. (2005) during the last decade. Actually, many sentence alignment methods were designed for related languages. The length-based alignment method in Gale and Church (1993) was originally intended for the related languages of English, French and German. The method of Kay and Roscheisen (1993) which uses a partial alignment of lexical items (cognates) to perform sentence alignment is also meant to be used for languages close to each other in the phylogenetic sense.

But directly aligning fairly dissimilar languages with different writing systems still remains a challenging task. For example, this could explain why the size of the Greek-English parallel corpus is one of the smallest corpora for the same time-span (1996-2011) in the Europarl Parallel Corpus, since the Greek language does not share the writing system of the other languages in the European Union. To explore the alignment of languages using different writing systems, Wu (1994) applies the method of Gale and Church (1993) to a parallel corpus between Cantonese and English from the Hong Kong Hansard using lexical cues, and Haruno and Yamazaki (1996) which is a variant of Kay and Roscheisen (1993) uses statistical and dictionary information for a parallel corpus between Japanese and English.

Accordingly, Moore (2002) and Varga et al. (2005) used partial translation models. Moore (2002) introduced a modified version of the well-known IBM Translation Model 1 using the highest probability 1-to-1 bids from the initial alignment. Varga et al. (2005) produced a crude translation

[2]See Zhang et al. (2017), as an exception.

of the source text using an existing bilingual dictionary. It seems natural that a translation model should be of precious help to align languages with different writing systems.

In this paper, we extend the length-based Gale and Church sentence alignment algorithm. The proposed algorithm is detailed in Hong (2013). Let $D(i, j)$ be the minimum distance. This is computed by minimizing operations as defined in Gale and Church (1993). We use the distance function d with six arguments s_1, t_1, s_2, t_2, s_3, t_3 instead of first four arguments. This is to extend to grouping up to three sentences, instead of two. Semantics of calculating $d(\cdot)$ is described in Figure 2. For example, $d(s_1, t_1; s_2, t_2; s_3, t_3)$ designates the cost of merging s_1, s_2, s_3 and matching with t_1, t_2, t_3. $\lambda_1 = 0.04, \lambda_2 = 0.21, \lambda_3 = 0.75$ are empirically estimated from the existing English-Korean parallel corpus, where $\sum_i \lambda_i = 1$.

3.3 Self-training method

We use a translation model learned from a previous alignment to produce an improved alignment at both document and sentence levels. This kind of practice is often called self-training (McClosky et al., 2006), self-taught learning (Raina et al., 2007), and lightly-supervised training (Schwenk, 2008). We assume that the initial, baseline translation models are trained with "out-domain" corpus, while the self-trained models are trained with "in-domain" corpus. Self-training therefore performs domain-adaptation that is beneficial to the quality of the final alignments.

At first, we translate Korean (C_k into English ($C^0_{k'}$) using the machine translation (MT) system trained with the pre-existing Korean-English bilingual corpus, as noted by $MT(BC^0_{\text{KoEN}})$. We then align documents and sentences to produce the parallel text for *translated* Korean and English. By restoring the original Korean sentences from translated Korean ($C^0_{k'}$) we build a new parallel corpus (BC^1_{KoEN}). From here, we can train a new MT system by adding the newly aligned bilingual corpus ($MT(BC^0_{\text{KoEN}} + BC^1_{\text{KoEN}})$) and re-translate Korean into English to build a self-trained BC^2_{KoEN}. This procedure can be summarized as follows:

1. Build a translation model using the existing parallel corpus $MT(BC^0_{\text{KoEN}})$.
2. Translate Korean C_k into English $C^0_{k'}$ using $MT(BC^0_{\text{KoEN}})$.
3. Align $C^0_{k'}$ and C_e.
4. Restore $C^0_{k'}$ to Korean and create a new parallel corpus BC^1_{KoEN}.
5. Build a new translation model by adding the newly aligned parallel corpus $MT(BC^0_{\text{KoEN}} + BC^1_{\text{KoEN}})$.
6. Repeat from (2) to (4) to create a self-trained parallel corpus BC^2_{KoEN}.

Through self-training, we can improve the translation quality for $C^i_{k'}$ and finally obtain better alignment results. Therefore, $C^i_{k'}$ (translation by $MT(\sum_i BC^i_{\text{KoEN}})$) and BC^{i+1}_{KoEN} are the corpora produced during self-training where $i = 0, 1$.

Figure 3 shows examples of English-Korean self-training. It shows their *intermediate* translation for original Korean sentences by the initial translation model and self-trained translation model. It is clear that the self-trained translation model is reinforced by the previously aligned corpus in which it provides more context-proper translation.

4 Experiments and Results

In this section, we detail our experiments and present our alignment results obtained through machine translation and self-training[3].

4.1 Data and systems

We experiment on a corpus extracted through web crawling. The corpus consists of news-wire articles from the *Dong-a Ilbo* website (literally 'East Asia Daily'). We obtained articles published during 2010 and 2011. It amounts to 3,249 documents for both Korean and English, containing 47,069 and 46,998 sentences respectively.

As far as non-linguistic preprocessing is concerned, we perform corpus cleaning using simple regular expressions after detecting text bodies. Since most contemporary HTML documents are created and edited by an HTML-specialized editor, we can easily detect the beginning and the end of text bodies in the document. Then, we can use the following regular expression to remove remaining HTML tags: `cat filename | sed "s/<[^>]*>//g"`. We empirically found that

[3]All obtained aligned data including source data (non-aligned original data) are made publicly available for further research.

$$D(i,j) = \min \begin{cases} D(i,j-1) + d(0,t_j;0,0;0,0) \\ D(i-1,j) + d(s_i,0;0,0;0,0) \\ D(i-1,j-1) + d(s_i,t_j;0,0;0,0) \\ D(i-1,j-2) + d(s_i,t_j;0,t_{j-1};0,0) \\ D(i-2,j-1) + d(s_i,t_j;s_{j-1},0;0,0) \\ D(i-2,j-2) + d(s_i,t_j;s_{j-1},t_{j-1};0,0) \\ D(i-1,j-3) + d(s_i,t_j;0,t_{j-1};0,t_{j-2}) \\ D(i-3,j-1) + d(s_i,t_j;s_{j-1},0;s_{j-2},0) \\ D(i-2,j-3) + d(s_i,t_j;s_{j-1},t_{j-1};0,t_{j-2}) \\ D(i-3,j-2) + d(s_i,t_j;s_{j-1},t_{j-1};s_{j-2},0) \\ D(i-3,j-3) + d(s_i,t_j;s_{j-1},t_{j-1};s_{j-2},t_{j-2}) \end{cases}$$

$$d(s_1,t_1;s_2,t_2;s_3,t_3) = \lambda_1 \log_2 Prob(\delta|match) + \lambda_2 + \lambda_3 \text{ cosine}(s_1+s_2+s_3, t_1+t_2+t_3)$$

Figure 2: Minimum distance

문화재청이 복원된 광화문의 현판 제막식을 갖고 광화문을 공개한 15일 광화문을 관람하려는 시민들의 발길이 하루 종일 이어졌다.
이날 오전 서울 광화문광장에서 열린 제65주년 광복절 경축식이 끝난 뒤 광화문을 지나 경복궁으로 들어가고 있는 시민들.
경복궁관리소는 이날 광화문을 찾은 시민이 10만여 명에 달한다고 밝혔다.

(a) Original Korean sentences

The Cultural restored Kwanghwamun's happened 제막식 Gwanghwamun, and released clockwise to watch the 15 days to citizens of 종일 a day.
Earlier in the day, Seoul's 광화문광장 65 anniversary of Liberation Day Changchung Gymnasium for after clockwise to Gyeongbok into and citizens.
The 경복궁관리소 clockwise to find the 10 million people.

(b) Translation from Korean into English by the initial MT model (MT^0)

The Cultural Heritage Administration laser-based traditional gate of a plate-hanging ceremony Sunday morning to the public 15 Gwanghwamun on to citizens of the Yeonyang.
At Gwanghwamun Plaza, the 65th Liberation Day after the gate into Gyeongbok Palace, and citizens.
The palace's management office under the the gate 10 million people 201,800 said.

(c) Translation after self-training (MT^1)

People flock to the restored gate of Gwanghwamun on Liberation Day Sunday.
The royal palace gate was opened to the public after a plate-hanging ceremony in the morning.
After a ceremony for the 65th Liberation Day at Gwanghwamun Plaza, people pass the traditional gate to enter Gyeongbok Palace.
The palace's office said more than 100,000 people visited the gate.

(d) Original English sentences

Figure 3: Examples of self-training

the proposed regular expression followed by manual detection of text bodies performs better than that the use of specific web page cleaning tools. This is especially true for web pages of *Donga Ilbo*, which require only one iteration of manual tagging, we can easily detect body parts which have the same structures for all documents. However, our method can be generalized by using such tools in future research.

After extracting text parts, sentence boundaries are detected using the ESPRESSO[4] POS tagger for Korean and SPLITTA described in Gillick (2009)[5] for English. We use these sentence segmented documents for document and sentence alignments. Then, we tokenize sentences using different methods depending on the language. As described before, we use the POS tagging system to tokenize Korean sentences and during the sentence segmentation task, tokenization is also performed. We use MOSES's tokenization script for English sentences. We also change the case of letters based on true case models for English.

For document alignment, we use LDA implemented in MALLET[6] to extract topic models. We convert the topics of each document into a single vector. We measure cosine similarity between two documents in different languages. Since we are working on English and English-translated Korean, we don't need polylingual topic models. For sentence alignment, we use a sentence alignment tool based on Hong (2013), which extends the algorithm of Gale and Church (1993). This sentence aligner enables the alignment of translated sentences and to restoration of original sentences based on sentence positions.

For Korean-English translation, we build the initial phrase-based statistical machine translation system using Korean parallel data that we previously collected from several bilingual Korean newswire sites. We do so with the Moses (Koehn et al., 2007) toolkit.[7] For alignment, we limit sentence length to 80 and use GIZA++ (Och and Ney, 2003). We use the SRILM (Stolcke, 2002) toolkit with Chen and Goodman's modified Kneser-Ney discounting for 5-grams for language model estimation. We also use `grow-diag-final-and` and `msd-bidirectional-fe` heuristics.[8] Finally, we use minimum error rate training (MERT) (Och, 2003) to tune the weights of the log-linear model.

[4]https://doi.org/10.5281/zenodo.884606

[5]https://code.google.com/p/splitta

[6]http://mallet.cs.umass.edu

[7]While we tested with a neural MT (NMT) system (Klein et al., 2017), the proposed method by SMT outperformed results from state-of-the-art NMT, most likely because of the small size of parallel data. We leave for future work the comparison of performance/results between statistical and neural systems with a bigger English-Korean bitext.

	Korean	MT^0	MT^1
precision	-	0.9701	0.9987
recall	-	0.9408	0.9981
F_1	-	0.9552	0.9984

Table 2: Results on document alignment

4.2 Results on document alignment

For the evaluation of document alignment, we use the name of documents as gold standard. Since the name of documents are identical for the Korean-English paired documents, for example 20101003K for Korean and 20101003E, we use this information as gold reference. Results on document alignment presented in this section are purely based on our proposed method that makes use of a topic model without referring to the name of documents. We evaluate our proposed methods using standard precision and recall as follows:

$$\begin{aligned}&\text{Precision}\\&=\frac{\text{\# of correctly paired documents}}{\text{\# of produced alignment by threshold}}\\&\text{Recall}\\&=\frac{\text{\# of correctly paired documents}}{\text{\# of total paired documents}}\end{aligned} \tag{3}$$

We report F_1 score based on precision and recall ($\frac{2PR}{P+R}$). Table 2 shows results on document alignment. We denote MT^0 for $MT(BC^0_{\text{KoEn}})$ and MT^1 for $MT(BC^0_{\text{KoEn}} + BC^1_{\text{KoEn}})$ for convenience' sake. We introduce a threshold $\theta \geq 0.5$ of similarity for document alignment. Empirically we found that the recall drops if the threshold is set too high. For example, obtaining a precision of 1 comes with a drop in recall of 25% from $\theta \geq 0.7$ to ≥ 0.8. By using the proposed method, we obtain up to 99.84% F1 score.

4.3 Results on sentence alignment

To evaluate sentence alignment, we manually align sentences to build a gold standard. We se-

[8]`http://www.statmt.org/moses/?n=Moses.Baseline` for more details.

	Korean	MT^0	MT^1
sent	37,333	39,209	38,802
tok	1,193,514	1,193,509	1,193,507

Table 3: Size of sentence alignment: (sent) for the number of sentences and (tok) for tokens in the English-side corpus.

	Korean	MT^0	MT^1
P	0.4943	0.5547	0.5575
R	0.5385	0.5874	0.5927
F_1	0.5154	0.5705	0.5746

Table 4: Results on sentence alignment

lect documents over a period of two months (documents from March and April 2010). It contains over 1,500 sentences for each language from 122 documents. We evaluate our proposed methods using precision and recall as before:

$$P = \frac{\text{\# of correct bids}}{\text{\# of produced bids}}, R = \frac{\text{\# of correct bids}}{\text{\# of total bids}} \quad (4)$$

Table 3 shows the size and results on sentence alignment. We report overall precision, recall and F_1 scores. We provide results on sentence alignment without translation in which sentence alignment is based on sentence length only (Korean). MT^0 is for alignment by translation and MT^1 is for alignment by self-training. Table 5 present results for each bid by MT^1 and their occurrences in the evaluation data. Bids represent Korean:English. We found that many Korean sentences are not translated into English and the proposed sentence alignment method can correctly detect them. Some errors occur in 1:1 bids because the alignment method have a tendency to merge adjacent sentences, it can show better results in higher bids such as $n : m$ where $n, m > 1$.

Finally, we perform an extrinsic evaluation of alignment quality by evaluating a machine translation system. We train with the newly aligned corpus and evaluate the translation model using the JHE evaluation data (Junior High English evaluation data for Korean-English machine translation)[9] and the Korean-English News parallel corpus[10].

[9] https://doi.org/10.5281/zenodo.891295

[10] https://github.com/jungyeul/korean-parallel-corpora

The direction of translation is Korean into English. Table 6 shows results using the translation quality metric BLEU (Papineni et al., 2002)[11].

5 Discussion on the Proposed Method

In this section, we first discuss the generalization of our proposed method, so that it does not get limited to the current bilingual setting. In the multilingual setting, we assume that we aim at aligning the source language and any other target language. We assume that there is a pivot language. Notations for this trilingual setting are described in Table 7. We use some analogy that we described for the bilingual setting in Table 1, such as C_k for the source language corpus (*e.g* Korean), C_e for the pivot language (English), and in addition C_f for the target language corpus (say, French).

Let k and f be Korean and French, respectively. English is a pivot language. We can use the result from the bilingual setting for the Korean to English translation to translate Korean into English. Then, we translate French into English using a MT system trained with a pre-existing French-English bilingual corpus. Finally, we align documents and sentences using English translated Korean-French documents to produce the parallel corpus by restoring the original Korean and French sentences. In the trilingual setting, we can also align French and English to improve the translation quality from French into English by providing a self-trained aligned corpus as we perform for Korean-English alignment. This procedure can be summarized as follows:

1. Create a self-trained parallel corpus BC^n_{KE} using the bilingual setting and build a translation model MT^n_{KE}.
2. Translate Korean C_k into English $C_{k'}$ using MT^n_{KE}.
3. Build a translation model using the existing parallel corpus $MT(BC^0_{\text{FE}})$.
4. Translate French C_f into English $C^0_{k'}$ using $MT(BC^0_{\text{FE}})$.
5. Align $C_{k'}$ and $C^0_{f'}$.
6. Restore $C_{k'}$ and and $C^0_{f'}$ to Korean and create a new parallel corpus BC^1_{KF}.

[11] ftp://jaguar.ncsl.nist.gov/mt/resources/mteval-v13a-20091001.tar.gz

	0:1	1:0	1:1	1:2	1:3	2:1	2:2	2:3	3:1	3:2	3:3
F_1	1.0	1.0	0.3552	0.7350	0.625	0.4761	0.8333	0.5	0.6667	1.0	1.0
occurrences	2	36	822	117	8	42	18	2	3	2	2

Table 5: Final results on sentence alignment for each bid for MT^1

	Ko	MT^0	MT^1	
w/o (BC^0_{KoEN})	4.10	4.39	4.55	JHE
with (BC^0_{KoEN})	7.47	8.03	**8.33**	JHE
with (BC^0_{KoEN})	9.17	9.35	**9.38**	News

Table 6: Results on sentence alignment by BLEU scores. Ko is for results of the baseline system where the corpus is aligned with the pivot language. We also perform the translation with and without the initial bilingual corpus BC^0.

7. Align $C_{f'}$ and C_e.
8. Restore $C^0_{f'}$ to French and create a new parallel corpus BC^1_{FE}.
9. Build a new translation model by adding the newly aligned parallel corpus $MT(BC^0_{FE} + BC^1_{FE})$.
10. Repeat from (3) to (9) to create a self-trained parallel corpus BC^i_{KF}.

Through self-training, we can improve the translation quality for $C_{f'}$ by using the self-trained French-English parallel corpus BC_{FE}. Finally, we obtain better alignment results between Korean and French thanks to the better translation $C_{f'}$. Practically, it would be difficult to apply the proposed generalized method to real data because of the lack of proper multilingual data for Korean. We are aware that there are some multilingual data for Korean such as technical documents and movie/tv-show subtitles (Some of them are already available at OPUS).[12] According to our previous experience, these types of corpora are relatively easy to align because they may contain lexical cues (technical terms) or time stamps (subtitles).

6 Conclusion and Future Perspectives

We explored the possibility of using a pivot language for the purpose of aligning two dissimilar languages. Results show that alignment as evaluated directly by document and sentence alignments or indirectly by translation quality (BLEU), is improved as compared with directly aligning those two languages. Applying the generalized method for other language pairs such as Greek-English in the Europarl parallel corpus, in which multilingual parallel data are available and Greek does not share the same writing system with other European languages, can be considered as future work. In addition to using the pivot language, we also built a better parallel corpus using self-trained translation models. For immediate future work, we continue to identify suitable bilingual/multilingual web sites to collect more parallel data for Korean.

Acknowledgments

The authors would like to thank the anonymous reviewers for their valuable comments and effort to improve the manuscript. J. Park and L. Dugast would like to thank Kyung Min Shin for the KOREANA bilingual data. This research was supported by Basic Science Research Program through the National Research Foundation of Korea (NRF) funded by the Ministry of Education (2017R1D1A1B03033534) for C.-U. Shin and J.-W. Cha.

References

David M. Blei, Andrew Y. Ng, and Michael I. Jordan. 2003. Latent Dirichlet Allocation. *Journal of Machine Learning Research* 3(4-5):993–1022.

Peter F. Brown, Jennifer C. Lai, and Robert L. Mercer. 1991. Aligning Sentences in Parallel Corpora. In *Proceedings of the 29th Annual Meeting of the Association for Computational Linguistics*. Association for Computational Linguistics, Berkeley, California, USA, pages 169–176. https://doi.org/10.3115/981344.981366.

Stanley F. Chen. 1993. Aligning Sentences in Bilingual Corpora using Lexical Information. In *Proceedings of the 31st Annual Meeting of the Association for Computational Linguistics*. Association for Computational Linguistics, Columbus, Ohio, USA, pages 9–16. https://doi.org/10.3115/981574.981576.

[12] `http://opus.lingfil.uu.se`

Description	Notation
Source language corpus	C_k
Pivot language translated source language corpus	$C^i_{k'}$, where $0 \leq i < n$
Target language corpus	C_f
Pivot language translated target language corpus	$C^i_{f'}$, where $0 \leq i < n$
Pivot language corpus	C_e
Bilingual Source-Pivot corpus	BC^i_{KE}, where $0 \leq i \leq n$
Bilingual Target-Pivot corpus	BC^i_{FE}, where $0 \leq i \leq n$
Bilingual Source-Target corpus	BC^i_{KF}, where $0 < i \leq n$
Source-Pivot MT system	$MT(\sum_i BC^i_{\text{KE}})$
Target-Pivot MT system	$MT(\sum_i BC^i_{\text{FE}})$

Table 7: Notations for the Multilingual Setting

William A. Gale and Kenneth W. Church. 1993. A Program for Aligning Sentences in Bilingual Corpora. *Computational Linguistics* 19(1):75–102.

Dan Gillick. 2009. Sentence Boundary Detection and the Problem with the U.S. In *Proceedings of Human Language Technologies: The 2009 Annual Conference of the North American Chapter of the Association for Computational Linguistics, Companion Volume: Short Papers*. Association for Computational Linguistics, Boulder, Colorado, pages 241–244. http://www.aclweb.org/anthology/N/N09/N09-2061.

Masahiko Haruno and Takefumi Yamazaki. 1996. High-Performance Bilingual Text Alignment Using Statistical and Dictionary Information. In *Proceedings of the 34th Annual Meeting of the Association for Computational Linguistics*. Association for Computational Linguistics, Santa Cruz, California, USA, pages 131–138. https://doi.org/10.3115/981863.981881.

Jeen-Pyo Hong. 2013. *Multilingual sentence alignment using translation models*. Ph.D. thesis, Changwon National University.

Martin Kay and Martin Roscheisen. 1993. Text-Translation Alignment. *Computational Linguistics* 19(1):121–142.

Guillaume Klein, Yoon Kim, Yuntian Deng, Jean Senellart, and Alexander Rush. 2017. OpenNMT: Open-Source Toolkit for Neural Machine Translation. In *Proceedings of ACL 2017, System Demonstrations*. Association for Computational Linguistics, Vancouver, Canada, pages 67–72. http://aclweb.org/anthology/P17-4012.

Philipp Koehn, Hieu Hoang, Alexandra Birch, Chris Callison-Burch, Marcello Federico, Nicola Bertoldi, Brooke Cowan, Wade Shen, Christine Moran, Richard Zens, Chris Dyer, Ondrej Bojar, Alexandra Constantin, and Evan Herbst. 2007. Moses: Open Source Toolkit for Statistical Machine Translation. In *Proceedings of the 45th Annual Meeting of the Association for Computational Linguistics Companion Volume Proceedings of the Demo and Poster Sessions*. Association for Computational Linguistics, Prague, Czech Republic, pages 177–180. http://www.aclweb.org/anthology/P07-2045.

David McClosky, Eugene Charniak, and Mark Johnson. 2006. Reranking and Self-Training for Parser Adaptation. In *Proceedings of the 21st International Conference on Computational Linguistics and 44th Annual Meeting of the Association for Computational Linguistics*. Association for Computational Linguistics, Sydney, Australia, pages 337–344. https://doi.org/10.3115/1220175.1220218.

Robert C. Moore. 2002. Fast and Accurate Sentence Alignment of Bilingual Corpora. In Stephen D. Richardson, editor, *Proceedings of the 5th Conference of the Association for Machine Translation in the Americas on Machine Translation: From Research to Real Users*. Springer-Verlag, Tiburon, CA, USA, pages 135–244.

Franz Josef Och. 2003. Minimum Error Rate Training in Statistical Machine Translation. In *Proceedings of the 41st Annual Meeting of the Association for Computational Linguistics*. Association for Computational Linguistics, Sapporo, Japan, pages 160–167. https://doi.org/10.3115/1075096.1075117.

Franz Josef Och and Hermann Ney. 2003. A Systematic Comparison of Various Statistical Alignment Models. *Computational Linguistics* 29(1):19–51.

Kishore Papineni, Salim Roukos, Todd Ward, and Wei-Jing Zhu. 2002. Bleu: a Method for Automatic Evaluation of Machine Translation. In *Proceedings of 40th Annual Meeting of the Association for Computational Linguistics*. Association for Computational Linguistics, Philadelphia, Pennsylvania, USA, pages 311–318. https://doi.org/10.3115/1073083.1073135.

Rajat Raina, Alexis Battle, Honglak Lee, Benjamin Packer, and Andrew Y Ng. 2007. Self-taught Learning: Transfer Learning from Unlabeled Data. In *Proceedings of the 24th International Conference on Machine Learning*. ACM, New York, NY, USA, ICML '07, pages 759–766. https://doi.org/10.1145/1273496.1273592.

Holger Schwenk. 2008. Investigations on Large-Scale Lightly-Supervised Training for Statistical Machine Translation. In *Proceedings of the International Workshop on Spoken Language Translation*. Hawaii, USA, pages 182–189.

Andreas Stolcke. 2002. SRILM - An Extensible Language Modeling Toolkit. In *Proceedings of the 7th International Conference on Spoken Language Processing, ICSLP2002 - INTERSPEECH 2002*. Denver, Colorado, pages 901–904.

Dániel Varga, Lázló Németh, Péter Halácsy, András Kornai, Viktor Trón, and Viktor Nagy. 2005. Parallel corpora for medium density languages. In *Proceedings of the RANLP (Recent Advances in Natural Language Processing)*. Borovets, Bulgaria, pages 590–596.

Dekai Wu. 1994. Aligning a Parallel English-Chinese Corpus Statistically with Lexical Criteria. In *Proceedings of the 32nd Annual Meeting of the Association for Computational Linguistics*. Association for Computational Linguistics, Las Cruces, New Mexico, USA, pages 80–87. https://doi.org/10.3115/981732.981744.

Hua Wu and Haifeng Wang. 2007. Pivot Language Approach for Phrase-Based Statistical Machine Translation. In *Proceedings of the 45th Annual Meeting of the Association of Computational Linguistics*. Association for Computational Linguistics, Prague, Czech Republic, pages 856–863. http://www.aclweb.org/anthology/P07-1108.

Hua Wu and Haifeng Wang. 2009. Revisiting Pivot Language Approach for Machine Translation. In *Proceedings of the Joint Conference of the 47th Annual Meeting of the ACL and the 4th International Joint Conference on Natural Language Processing of the AFNLP*. Association for Computational Linguistics, Suntec, Singapore, pages 154–162. http://www.aclweb.org/anthology/P/P09/P09-1018.

Meng Zhang, Yang Liu, Huanbo Luan, and Maosong Sun. 2017. Adversarial Training for Unsupervised Bilingual Lexicon Induction. In *Proceedings of the 55th Annual Meeting of the Association for Computational Linguistics (Volume 1: Long Papers)*. Association for Computational Linguistics, Vancouver, Canada, pages 1959–1970. http://aclweb.org/anthology/P17-1179.

MultiNews:
A Web collection of an Aligned Multimodal and Multilingual Corpus

Haithem Afli, Pintu Lohar and Andy Way
ADAPT Centre
School of Computing
Dublin City University
Dublin, Ireland
{FirstName.LastName}@adaptcentre.ie

Abstract

Integrating Natural Language Processing (NLP) and computer vision is a promising effort. However, the applicability of these methods directly depends on the availability of a specific multimodal data that includes images and texts. In this paper, we present a collection of a Multimodal corpus of comparable document and their images in 9 languages from the web news articles of Euronews website.[1] This corpus has found widespread use in the NLP community in Multilingual and multimodal tasks. Here, we focus on its acquisition of the images and text data and their multilingual alignment.

1 Introduction

Although many Natural Language Processing (NLP) applications can be developed by using existing corpora, there are many areas where NLP could be useful if there was a suitable corpus available. For example, Multimodal Machine Translation and Crosslingual Image Description Generation tasks [2] are becoming interested in developing methods that can use not only the texts but also their relations with images. Such information can neither be obtained from standard computer vision data sets such as the COREL collection [3]nor from NLP collections such as Europarl [4] (Koehn, 2005). Similarly, although the image near a text article on a website may provide cues about finding more monolingual and multilingual comparable documents and information on the same topic of the article. We therefore set out to collect a corpus of images aligned with simple full-sentence texts in different languages.

This paper describes our experiences with acquising and aligning multimodal data. Although we did not set out to run a scientific experiment comparing different strategies of how to collect images and texts, our experience points towards certain recommendations for how to collect data for computer vision and NLP domains from news websites such Euronews.

2 Building Multimodal and Multilingual Corpus

The construction of a multilingual corpus for the use in a NLP application typically takes five steps:

(i) obtain the raw data (e.g., web pages)

(ii) align the articles (document alignment)

(iii) extract the texts

(iv) prepare the corpus for NLP applications (normalisation, tokenisation)

(v) map sentences/phrases in one language sentences in the other language (parallel data extraction) In the following, we will describe in detail the acquisition of the Euronews corpus from the website of Euronews.

In this work, data is extracted from the available news (image and text modalities) on the *Euronews* website.[5] Figure 1 shows an example of multimodal comparable data coming from the *Euronews* website. An image source of a political news item and its text version – both in English

[1] euronews.com

[2] statmt.org/wmt16/multimodal-task.html

[3] The COREL Database for COntent based image REtrievaL https://sites.google.com/site/dctresearch/Home/content-based-image-retrieval

[4] www.statmt.org/europarl/

[5] http://www.euronews.com

Proceedings of the Workshop on Curation and Applications of Parallel and Comparable Corpora, pages 11–15,
Taipei, Taiwan, November 27–December 1, 2017. ©2017 AFNLP

Figure 1: Example of comparable documents from the *Euronews* Web site.

– are available along with the equivalent news in French (image and text modalities). These documents can be used to extract comparable documents and parallel data.

Euronews web site clusters news into several categories including languages and sub-domains (*e.g.* Sport, Politics, etc.). Table 2 shows the statistics of our *MMEuronews* corpus created from news article data from 2013, 2014 and 2105 in 9 languages including: fr(French), ar(Arabic), en(English), de(German), es(Spanish), it(Italian), tr(Turkish), ua(Ukrainian), and pt(Portuguese).

3 Aligning Comparable documents

3.1 Basic Idea

We propose an extension of the method described in (Sennrich and Volk, 2010) to align our corpus. The basic system architecture is described in Figure 2. We begin by removing the documents that have very little contents in order to reduce the total number of all possible comparisons. Such documents are very rarely considered as candidates for being comparable document because they consist of only few sentences or words and it is observed that in the reference for training data provided, these kind of documents are not included in the reference set. Subsequently, we introduced three methods as follows: (i) sentence-level scoring, (ii) word-level scoring, and (iii) named entity (NE)-based scoring.

Finally we added these three scores to select the 1-best target document which has the highest value.

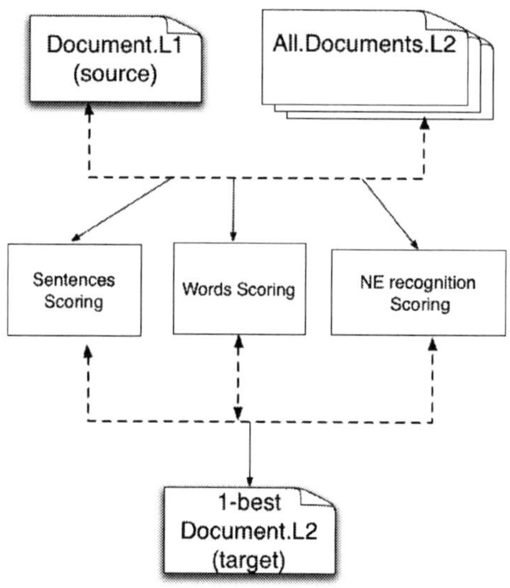

Figure 2: Architecture of comparable alignment system alignment

Language	en	fr	ar	de	es	it	pt	tr	ua	Total
# Articles	40421	39663	36836	37293	37218	36970	36854	37291	37021	339 567

Table 1: Size of the Euronews transcribed English audio corpus and English-French texts.

3.2 Sentence based scoring

Since there are a large number of source and target documents especially in the domains with with a large amount of documents, we have to restrict the comparison process only to the source-target document pairs that have close sentence-length ratio. Otherwise they are very less likely to be comparable documents. It is necessary since comparing each source with each target document would result in an undesirably large number of comparisons($m * n$, with m and n being the total number of source and target documents, respectively in a specific domain) and therefore very long time for the whole computation even for a single domain. Let us assume that S_s and S_t are number of sentences in source and target document respectively. Assuming this we follow very simple formula to calculate source-target sentence-length ratio(S_{LR}) as follows:

$$S_{LR} = \frac{Min(S_s, S_t)}{Max(S_s, S_t)} \quad (1)$$

We construct this equation in order to confine the value between 0 and 1 which implies that if either of source and target document has no sentences, S_{LR} will be 0 and 1 if they have same number of sentences. Therefore, a value of 1 or even very close to it has positive indication towards being comparable but this is not the only requirement as there are many documents with same or nearly same number of sentences. Due to this reason, we consider word and NE-based scorings in sections 3.4 and 3.5 respectively.

3.3 Word based scoring

The reason behind using this method is very similar to the method discussed in Section 3.2 except that it is used at word level. Let us assume that W_s and W_t are number of words in source and target documents respectively. Hence our equation for calculating source-target word-length ratio(W_{LR}) becomes:

$$W_{LR} = \frac{Min(W_s, W_t)}{Max(W_s, W_t)} \quad (2)$$

3.4 NE-based scoring

After a linguistic study on the comparable documents, we found that looking for NEs present in both source and target documents can be a good way to select the 1-best target document. We extracted NEs from all the documents to be compared and calculate the percentage of source NE matches(P_{SNM}) with target NEs.

However, in many cases a source and a target documents can have huge difference in number of NEs. For example, if a source document has 5 and a target document has 50 NEs respectively and all of the source NEs match with target NEs, it is probably a bad idea to simply calculate P_{SNM} and add to the sentence-based and to the word-based scores. Due to this reason we consider the source-target-NE-length ratio (NE_{LR}) and multiplied it with P_{SNM} . Hence the weight of P_{SNM} is decreased from 100% to 10% which is a result from depending upon N_{LR}. Henceforth, the NE-based score(NE_{SC}) is described as:

$$NE_{SC} = P_{SNM} * N_{LR} \quad (3)$$

3.5 Combining all scores

We propose to re-rank our possible alignments based on adding sentence, word and NE-based scores and call this as alignment-score (A_{SC})

$$A_{SC} = S_{LR} + W_{LR} + NE_{SC} \quad (4)$$

Using equation 4 we calculate scores for each document pairs in comparison and retain the 1-best pair that has the maximum value.

4 Results

The results are given in Table 2. Each row in the table contains three numerical values that represent (from left to right) the total numbers of source-language, target-language and aligned document pairs, respectively. As we can see, we are successfully aligning images and texts in 8 pair of languages. We produced a total of more than 288k of bilingual aligned multimodal documents. Our corpus, alignment model and code will be made

Documents	# Source	# Target	# Aligned
En-Ar	40421	36836	35761
En-De	40421	37293	36114
En-Es	40421	37218	36178
En-Fr	40421	37293	36762
En-It	40421	36970	36003
En-Pt	40421	36854	35863
En-Tr	40421	37291	35901
En-Ua	40421	37021	35922
Total			288 504

Table 2: Results of bilingual aligned image-text MMEuronews data used in our experiments.

publicly for the computer vision and NLP community.

5 Related Work on Document Alignment

In the "Big Data" world that we now live in, it is widely believed that *there is no better data than more data* (e.g. Mayer-Schönberger and Cukier (2013)). In line with this idea, many works use the Web as resource for building corpus for document alignment and parallel text extraction tasks. However, the extensive literature related to the problem of exploiting comparable corpora takes a somewhat different perspective than we do in this paper.

Typically, comparable corpora do not have any information regarding document pair similarity. They are made of many documents in one language which do not have any corresponding translated document in the other language. Furthermore, when the documents are paired, they are not literal translations one of each other. Thus, extracting parallel data from such corpora requires special algorithms.

Many works use the Web as a comparable corpus. An adaptive approach, proposed by Zhao and Vogel (2002), aims at mining parallel sentences from a bilingual comparable news collection collected from the Web. A maximum likelihood criterion was used by combining sentence-length models with lexicon-based models. The translation lexicon is iteratively updated using the mined parallel data to obtain better vocabulary coverage and translation probability estimation. Resnik and Smith (2003) propose a web-mining-based system called STRAND and show that their approach is able to find large numbers of similar document pairs. In (Yang and Li, 2003), an alignment method is presented at different levels (title, word and character) based on dynamic programming (DP). The goal is to identify one-to-one title pairs in an English–Chinese corpus collected from the Web. They apply the longest common subsequence to find the most reliable Chinese translation of an English word.

One of the main methods relies on cross-lingual information retrieval (CLIR), with different techniques for transferring the request into the target language (using a bilingual dictionary or a full SMT system). Utiyama and Isahara (2003) use CLIR techniques and DP to extract sentences from an English–Japanese comparable corpus. They identify similar article pairs, and having considered them as parallel texts, then align sentences using a sentence-pair similarity score and use DP to find the least-cost alignment over the document pair. (Munteanu and Marcu, 2005) use a bilingual lexicon to translate some of the words of the source sentence. These translations are then used to query the database to find matching translations using IR techniques.

There have been only a few studies trying to investigate the formal quantification of how similar two comparable documents are. Li and Gaussier (2010) presented one of the first works on developing a comparability measure based on the expectation of finding translation word pairs in the corpus. Our approach follows this line of work based on a method developed by Sennrich and Volk (2010).

6 Conclusion

Despite the fact that many researchers have investigated the use of comparable corpora to generate initial training data for NLP, we still have a lack of corpus in different modalities.

In this paper, we seek to build a corpus that combine aligned images and texts in different languages. We use Euronews website as source of our crawled raw data. We propose a new techniques to align bilingual documents. Our method is based on Matched source-to-target sentence/words and Named Entity scoring.

Given this promising result, in future work we would like to add more language pairs and data to our corpus. In addition, we wish to investigate its utility to improve the extraction of parallel data from multilingual comparable corpora. We plan, also, to develop a new model for building embeddings that are both multilingual and multimodal.

Finally, we hope that the availability of this kind of resources (corpora, tools) continues to make computer vision and NLP an exciting and productive fields.

Acknowledgments

This research is supported by Science Foundation Ireland through ADAPT Centre (Grant 13/RC/2106) (www.adaptcentre.ie) at Dublin City University.

References

Koehn, P. (2005). Europarl: A parallel corpus for statistical machine translation. *Proceedings of MT Summit.*

Li, B. and Gaussier, E. (2010). Improving corpus comparability for bilingual lexicon extraction from comparable corpora. In *Proceedings of the 23rd International Conference on Computational Linguistics (Coling 2010),*, pages 644–652.

Mayer-Schönberger, V. and Cukier, K. (2013). Big data: A revolution that will transform how we live, work, and think. In *London: Hodder & Stoughton.*

Munteanu, D. S. and Marcu, D. (2005). Improving Machine Translation Performance by Exploiting Non-Parallel Corpora. *Computational Linguistics*, 31(4):477–504.

Resnik, P. and Smith, N. A. (2003). The web as a parallel corpus. *Comput. Linguist.*, 29:349–380.

Sennrich, R. and Volk, M. (2010). Mt-based sentence alignment for ocr-generated parallel texts. In *The Ninth Conference of the Association for Machine Translation in the Americas (AMTA 2010).*

Utiyama, M. and Isahara, H. (2003). Reliable measures for aligning japanese-english news articles and sentences. In *Proceedings of the 41st Annual Meeting on Association for Computational Linguistics - Volume 1*, ACL '03, pages 72–79.

Yang, C. C. and Li, K. W. (2003). Automatic construction of english/chinese parallel corpora. *J. Am. Soc. Inf. Sci. Technol.*, 54:730–742.

Zhao, B. and Vogel, S. (2002). Adaptive parallel sentences mining from web bilingual news collection. In *Proceedings of the 2002 IEEE International Conference on Data Mining*, ICDM '02, Washington, DC, USA. IEEE Computer Society.

Learning Phrase Embeddings from Paraphrases with GRUs

Zhihao Zhou and **Lifu Huang** and **Heng Ji**

Rensselaer Polytechnic Institute
{zhouz5, huangl7, jih}@rpi.edu

Abstract

Learning phrase representations has been widely explored in many Natural Language Processing (NLP) tasks (e.g., Sentiment Analysis, Machine Translation) and has shown promising improvements. Previous studies either learn non-compositional phrase representations with general word embedding learning techniques or learn compositional phrase representations based on syntactic structures, which either require huge amounts of human annotations or cannot be easily generalized to all phrases. In this work, we propose to take advantage of large-scaled paraphrase database and present a pair-wise gated recurrent units (pairwise-GRU) framework to generate compositional phrase representations. Our framework can be re-used to generate representations for any phrases. Experimental results show that our framework achieves state-of-the-art results on several phrase similarity tasks.

1 Introduction

Continuous vector representations of words, also known as word embeddings, have been used as features for all kinds of NLP tasks such as Information Extraction (Lample et al., 2016; Zeng et al., 2014; Feng et al., 2016; Huang et al., 2016), Semantic Parsing (Chen and Manning, 2014; Zhou and Xu, 2015; Konstas et al., 2017), Sentiment Analysis (Socher et al., 2013b; Kalchbrenner et al., 2014; Kim, 2014; Tai et al., 2015), Question Answering (Tellex et al., 2003; Kumar et al., 2015) and machine translation (Cho et al., 2014; Zhang et al., 2014) and have yielded state-of-the-art results. However, single word embeddings are not enough to express natural languages. In many applications, we need embeddings for phrases. For example, in Information Extraction, we need representations for multi-word entity mentions, and in Question Answering, we may need representations for even longer question and answer phrases.

Generally, there are two types of models to learn phrase emmbeddings: noncompositional models and compositional models. Noncompositional models treat phrases as single information units while ignoring their components and structures. Embeddings of phrases can thus be learned with general word embedding learning techniques (Mikolov et al., 2013; Yin and Schütze, 2014; Yazdani et al., 2015), however, such methods are not scalable to all English phrases and suffer from data sparsity.

On the other hand, compositional models derives a phrase's embedding from the embeddings of its component words (Socher et al., 2012; Mikolov et al., 2013; Yu and Dredze, 2015; Poliak et al., 2017). Previous work have shown good results from compositional models which simply used predefined functions such as element-wise addition (Mikolov et al., 2013). However, such methods ignore word orders and cannot capture complex linguistic phenomena. Other studies on compositional models learn complex composition functions from data. For instance, the Recursive Neural Network (Socher et al., 2012) finds all linguistically plausible phrases in a sentence and recursively compose phrase embedding from subphrase embeddings with learned matrix/tensor transformations.

Since compositional models can derive embeddings for unseen phrases from word embeddings, they suffer less from data sparsity. However, the difficulty of training such complex compositional models lies in the choice of training data.

Proceedings of the Workshop on Curation and Applications of Parallel and Comparable Corpora, pages 16–23,
Taipei, Taiwan, November 27–December 1, 2017. ©2017 AFNLP

Although compositional models can be trained unsupervisedly with auto encoders such as the Recursive Auto Encoder (Socher et al., 2011), such models ignore contexts and actual usages of phrases and thus cannot fully capture the semantics of phrases. Some previous work train compositional models for a specific task, such as Sentiment Analysis (Socher et al., 2013b; Kalchbrenner et al., 2014; Kim, 2014) or syntactic parsing (Socher et al., 2010). But these methods require large amounts of human annotated data. Moreover, the embeddings obtained will be biased to a specific task and thus will not be applicable for other tasks. A more general source of training data which does not require human annotation is plain text through language modeling. For example, Yu and Dredze (2015) trained compositional models on bigram noun phrases with the language modeling objective. However, using the language modeling objective to train compositional models to compose every phrase in plain text would be impractical for large corpus.

In this work, we are aiming to tackle these challenges and generate more general and high-quality phrase embeddings. While it's impossible to provide "gold" annotation for the semantics of a phrase, we propose to take advantage of the large-scaled paraphrases, since the only criteria of determining two phrases are parallel is that they express the same meaning. This property can be naturally used as a training objective.

Considering this, we propose a general framework to train phrase embeddings on paraphrases. We designed a pairwise-GRU architecture, which consists of a pair of GRU encoders on two paraphrases. Our framework has much better generalizability. Although in this work, we only trained and tested our framework on short paraphrases, our model can be further applied to any longer phrases. We demonstrate the effectiveness of our framework on various phrase similarity tasks. Results show that our model can achieve state-of-the-art performance on capturing semantics of phrases.

2 Approach

In this section, we first introduce a large-scaled paraphrase database, the ParaPhrase DataBase (PPDB). Then, we show the basic GRU encoder and our pairwise-GRU based neural architecture. Finally, we provide the training details.

2.1 Paraphrase Database

PPDB (Ganitkevitch et al., 2013) is a database which contains hundreds of millions of English paraphrase pairs extracted from bilingual parallel corpora. It is constructed with the bilingual pivoting method (Bannard and Callison-Burch, 2005). Namely if two English phrases are translated to the same foreign phrase, then the two English phrases are considered to be paraphrases. PPDB comes with 6 pre-packaged sizes: S to XXXL [1]. In our work, to ensure efficiency and correctness, we only used the smallest and most accurate S package. To generate training data, we filtered out the paraphrases (p_1, p_2) where

1. p_1 is identical to p_2
2. p_1 or p_2 contains any non-letter characters except spaces
3. p_1 or p_2 contains words which are not contained in our trained word embeddings
4. p_1 and p_2 are both single words

After such a filtering step, we obtained a total number of 406,170 paraphrase pairs.

2.2 GRU Encoder

Recurrent neural networks have been proved to be very powerful models to encode natural language sequences. Because of the difficulty to train such networks on long sequences, extensions to the RNN architecture such as the long short-term memory (LSTM) (Hochreiter and Schmidhuber, 1997) and the gated recurrent units (GRU) (Cho et al., 2014) have been subsequently designed, which yielded even stronger performances. Gated structures allow models like the LSTM and the GRU to remember and forget inputs based on the gates' judgment of the inputs' importances, which in turn help the neural networks to maintain a more persistent memory.

The properties of such gated structures also make these models especially suitable for deriving phrase embeddings: for a compositional model to derive phrase embeddings from word embeddings, it is important that the model recognize words in each phrase which have more impact on the meaning of the phrase. For example, the embedding of "black cat" should be very close to the embedding of "cat". Thus the model should partially ignore

[1] http://paraphrase.org/

the word "black" and let the word "cat" dominate the final phrase embedding.

In this work, we chose our compositional model to be the GRU, since it was not only faster to train than the LSTM, but also slightly better-performing on our evaluation tasks. Mathematically, the j'th activation of the GRU at time step t, h_t^j, is given by:

$$h_t^j = (1 - z_t^j)h_{t-1}^j + z_t^j\widetilde{h}_t^j$$

where $\widetilde{h}_t^j$ is the current candidate activation and z_t^j is an update gate which dictates the extend to which the current activation is influenced by the current candidate activation and to which it maintains previous activation.

The candidate activation is given by:

$$\widetilde{h}_t^j = tanh(Wx_t + U(r_t \odot h_{t-1}))^j$$

where U and W are transformation matrices, x_t is the current input vector, and r_t is a vector of reset gates which controls how much the model forgets the previous activations.

The update gates and reset gates are both calculated based on the previous activations and current inputs:

$$z_t^j = \sigma(W_z x_t + U_z h_{t-1})^j$$

$$r_t^j = \sigma(W_r x_t + U_r h_{t-1})^j$$

Concretely, given the phrase "black cat", when it reads the word "cat", the GRU can learn to forget the word "black" by setting the update gates z_t close to 1 and setting the reset gates r_t close to 0. In this way the final phrase representation of the phrase will mostly be influenced by the word "cat".

2.3 PGRU: Pairwise-GRU

In order to train GRUs on paraphrases, we propose a Pairwise-GRU (*PGRU*) architecture, which contains two GRUs sharing the same weights, to encode each phrase in the paraphrase pair. Figure 1 shows the overview of our framework. Given a phrase pair (p_1, p_2), e.g., p_1 ="*chairman of the European observatory*" and p_2 ="*president of the European monitoring center*", we first initialize each token in each phrase with a pre-trained word embedding, then the two sequence of word embeddings are taken as input to two GRUs. We take the last hidden layers of the GRUs as the phrase embeddings of p_1 and p_2, and measure their similarity using cosine similarity with dot product.

Unlike the Recursive Neural Network (*Tree-RNN*) which maps phrases to the word embedding space (Socher et al., 2013b), the PGRU maps every phrase, including single words, to a separate phrase embedding space. This characteristic is very important for training the model on paraphrases. For example, given a paraphrase pair "America" and "the United States", the *Tree-RNN* only performs matrix/tensor transformations on the embeddings of "the United States", and generates a new vector representation which would ideally be close to the embedding of "America". However, since the embedding of "America" is kept constant, transformations on "the United States" has to be very complex.On the other hand, the PGRU uses GRUs to encode both "America" and "the United States" and make their phrase embeddings to be close to each other. Since neither embedding is aimed to be a predefined vector, the transformations can be much simpler and thus much easier to train.

2.4 Negative Sampling and Training Objectives

It is not enough for a model to map paraphrases to similar embeddings, since it is also important that it maps semantically different phrases to different embeddings. Thus we need to train the model to distinguish paraphrases from non-paraphrases. Similar to word embedding learning, we use negative sampling (Mikolov et al., 2013) to achieve this learning outcome. For each paraphrase pair (p_1, p_2), we select k contrast phrases $c_1, c_2, ..., c_k$ uniformly at random from the whole paraphrase database regardless of their frequencies of occurrence in the original corpora. Thus the goal of our model is, given the phrase p_1, correctly predict that p_2 is a paraphrase of p_1 and all contrast phrases $c_1, c_2, ..., c_k$ are not.

We chose our loss function to be the contrastive max-margin loss (Socher et al., 2013a). The main reasoning behind using this training objective is that while we want the cosine similarity of p_1 to its paraphrase p_2 to be high, it only has to be higher than the similarity of p_1 to any contrast phrase c_i by a certain margin so that the model can make correct predictions. Following Socher et al. (2013a), we set the margin to 1.

The contrastive max-margin loss for each train-

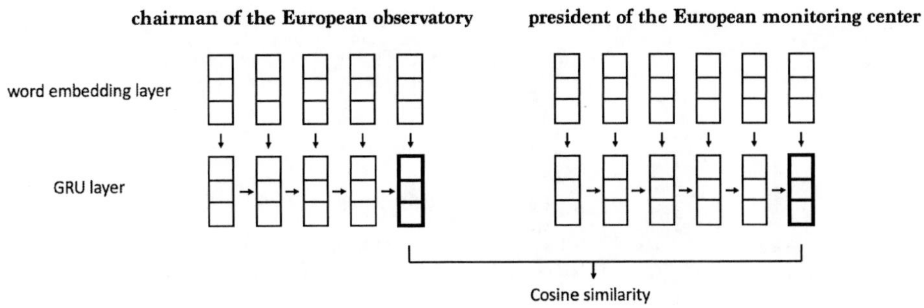

Figure 1: PGRU encodes phrase pairs with two GRUs which share the same parameters regardless of phrase lengths. Similarity is calculated by multiplying the two last hidden states with dot product.

ing example is defined as:

$$J_t(\theta) = \sum_{i=1}^{k} max(0, 1 - p_1^T p_2 + p_1^T c_i)$$

where p_1, p_2 and c_i are the embeddings of the paraphrases and contrast phrases respectively. And k is the number of contrast phrases.

And the overall loss is calculated by averaging objectives for all training examples:

$$J(\theta) = \frac{1}{T} \sum_{t=1}^{T} J_t(\theta)$$

where T is the number of training examples.

It is worth noting that, although previous embedding training work has predominantly used the negative sampling objective (Mikolov et al., 2013), the contrastive max-margin loss achieved much superior performances in our experiments.

2.5 Hyperparameters and Training Details

We used 200-dimensional word embeddings pretrained with word2vec (Mikolov et al., 2013). We set the number of hidden units of the GRU cell to 200 while using dropout (Hinton et al., 2012) with a dropout rate of 0.5 on the GRU cells to prevent overfitting. We also used gradient clipping (Pascanu et al., 2013; Graves, 2013) with maximum gradient norm set to 5. Training was accomplished with stochastic gradient descent (SGD) with a learning rate of 0.3, a minibatch size of 128 and a total number of epochs of 150.

3 Experiments

3.1 PPDB experiments

We randomly split the paraphrase pairs chosen from PPDB (as described in Section 2.1) to 80%, 10% and 10% as training, development and test sets. To see how the size of training data affects training results, we experimented training with 1%, 10% and 100% of our training set. We also experimented setting the number of contrast phrases k to 9, 29 and 99 for each training set size (which correspond to a 10/30/100 choose 1 task for the model). Finally, we evaluated the models trained under each configuration on our test set, where we set k to 99 and computed the accuracy of the model choosing a phrase's paraphrase among contrast phrases. More formally, for a test example $\{p_1, p_2, c_1, c_2, ..., c_k\}$, the models were given the phrase p_1 and asked to choose its paraphrase p_2 from the set $\{p_2, c_1, c_2, ..., c_k\}$.

To demonstrate the effectiveness of this training procedure, we also included the performance of the commonly used average encoder (*AVG*) on our test set. *AVG* simply takes the element-wise average of a phrase's component word embeddings as the phrase's embedding.

As shown in Figure 2, the commonly used *AVG* encoder achieved a score of 88%, which suggests that it is indeed a rather effective compositional model. But after adequate training on PPDB, *PGRU* is able to significantly improve upon *AVG*. This shows that *AVG* is not complex enough to fully capture semantics of phrases compared to complex compositional models like the GRU. It also suggests that, during PPDB training, our model can learn useful information about the meaning of phrases which were not learned by word embedding models during word embedding training. From the figure, we can also see consistent performance gain from adding more training data. This again proves that a large paraphrase database is useful for training compositional mod-

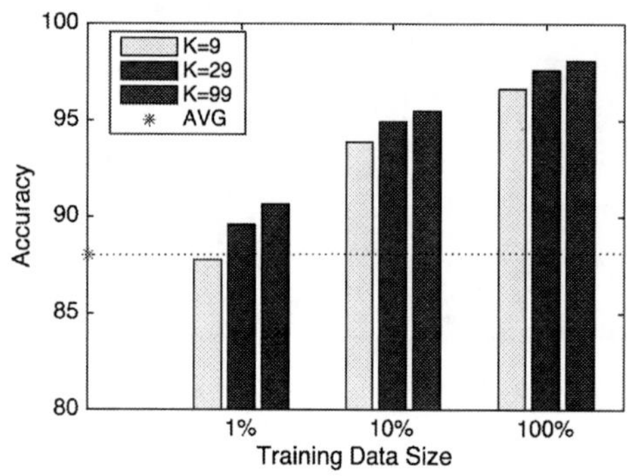

Figure 2: Performances of *PGRU* trained under different configurations as well as the performance of *AVG*.

els. Moreover, for each training set size, while we observe obvious performance gain from increasing k from 9 to 29, the gain from further increasing k to 99 is more moderate. Considering the amount of additional computation required, we conclude that it is not worth the computation efforts to increase k even further.

3.2 Phrase Similarity Tasks

Datasets

Following Yu and Dredze (2015), we evaluated our model on human annotated datasets including SemEval2013 Task 5(a) (**SemEval2013**) (Korkontzelos et al., 2013) and the noun-modifer problem in Turney2012 (**Turney2012**) (Turney, 2012). **SemEval2013** is a task to classify a phrase pair as either semantically similar or dissimilar. **Turney2012(5)** is a task to select the most semantically similar word to the given bigram phrase among 5 candidate words. In order to test the model's sensitivity to word orders, extended from **Turney2012(5)**, **Turney2012(10)** reverse the bigram and add it to the original bigram side. Thus the model needs to choose a bigram from these two bigrams and also choose the most semantically similar word from 5 candidates. Examples for these tasks are shown in Table 2.

Both tasks include separate training and evaluation sets. Note that although both tasks only contain unigram and bigram noun phrases, our approach of learning phrase embeddings can be applied to n-grams of any kind. We tested the performances of the GRU trained on the provided training set for each task (*GRU*) as well as the GRU trained only on the PPDB data (*GRU(PPDB)*), as described in Section 2. For task-unspecific training (*GRU(PPDB)*), we used the training set of each task as development set and applied early stopping.

Baselines

We compare our results against baseline results reported by Yu and Dredze (2015). The baseline method *SUM* is the commonly used elementwise addition method (Mitchell and Lapata, 2010). *RAE* is the recursive auto encoder (Socher et al., 2011) which is unsupervisedly trained to compose phrase embeddings such that the resulting phrase embeddings can be used predict the phrase's composing word embeddings. *FCT* (Yu and Dredze, 2015) is a compositional model which calculates a phrase's embeddings as a per-dimension weighted average of the component word embeddings while taking into consideration linguistic features such as part of speech tags. *FCT(LM)* (Yu and Dredze, 2015) is the FCT model trained on news corpus with language modeling objective instead of on the provided training sets for each task. *Tree-RNN* is the recursive neural network (Socher et al., 2011, 2013b) which builds up phrase embeddings from composing word embeddings with matrix transformations while also taking advantage of POS tags and parse tree structures.

We divide our results to comparisons of task-specific models and comparisons of task-unspecific ones, where for task-specific models, we remove scores from Yu and Dredze (2015) which require fine-tuning word embeddings since we are only comparing compositional models. For the sake of comparison, we use the same word embeddings used by Yu and Dredze (2015), although better scores can be achieved by using word embeddings of larger vocabulary size.

Results

As shown in table 1, *GRU* performs the best among all task-specific models in all three tasks, which proves that GRU is a very powerful compositional model and suggests that it is a suitable model to learn compositional phrase embeddings. *GRU*'s much superior performances on **Turney2012(5)** and **Turney2012(10)** can also be attributed to the fact that we used the contrastive max-margin loss (as described in Section 2.4) as training objective, which proved to be more effective in our experiments than the negative sampling

Model	Task Specific	SemEval2013	Turney2012(5)	Turney2012(10)
SUM	False	65.46	39.58	19.79
RAE	False	51.75	22.99	14.81
FCT(LM)	False	67.22	**42.59**	**27.55**
GRU(PPDB)	False	**71.29**	41.44	26.37
Tree-RNN	True	71.50	40.95	27.20
FCT	True	68.84	41.90	33.80
GRU	True	**73.44**	**48.88**	**39.23**

Table 1: Performances of our models and baselines on **SemEval2013**, **Turney2012(5)** and **Turney2012(10)**. Models are split into task-specific ones and task-unspecific ones for comparison.

Data Set	Input	Output	train/eval size
SemEval2013	(bomb, explosive device)	True	11722/7814
Turney2012	air current , {wind, gas, sedum, sudorific, bag}	wind	680/1500

Table 2: Examples for **SemEval2013** and **Turney2012** as well as the number of training and evaluation examples for each task.

objective used by Yu and Dredze (2015).

Among task-unspecific models, *GRU(PPDB)* also achieves strong performances. In all three tasks, *GRU(PPDB)* outperforms *SUM*, suggesting that the compositional model learned from PPDB can indeed be used for other domains and tasks. In particular, on **Turney2012(10)**, *GRU(PPDB)* improves upon *SUM* by a large margin. This is because unlike *SUM*, GRUs can capture the order of words in natural language. It also suggests that on tasks where word order plays an important role, using GRUs trained on PPDB can be more appropriate than using *SUM*. *GRU(PPDB)* also outperforms *FCT(LM)* on **SemEval2013** and achieves very close performances to *FCT(LM)* on **Turney2012(5)** and **Turney2012(5)** despite the fact that *FCT(LM)* is specifically designed and trained to compose noun phrases, which are the only type of phrases present in these three tasks, whereas our model works for all types of phrases. In addition, unlike the FCT, our method of training GRUs on paraphrases do not need any linguistic features produced by parsers which can be prone to errors.

4 Related Work

Phrase embeddings can be learned from either compositional or noncompositional models. Noncompositional models learn phrase embeddings by treating phrases as single units while ignoring their components and structures. But such methods are not scalable to all English phrases and suffer from data sparsity.

Compositional models build phrase embeddings from the embeddings of its component words. Previous work has shown that simple predefined composition functions such as elementwise addition (Mikolov et al., 2013) are relatively effective. However, such methods ignore word orders and are thus inadequate to capture complex linguistic phenomena.

One way to capture word order and other linguistic phenomena is to learn more complex composition functions from data. For instance, Recursive Neural Networks (Socher et al., 2011, 2013b) recursively compose embeddings of all linguistically plausible phrases in a parse tree with complex matrix/tensor transformation functions. However, models like this are very hard to train. When there are no human-annotations, we can train each phrase embedding to reconstruct the embeddings of it subphrases in the parse tree (Socher et al., 2011), but this objective does not capture the meaning of the phrase. When there are human-annotations, for example, if we have annotated sentiment score for each phrase, we can train the embeddings of phrases to predict their sentiment scores. However, in most cases, we do not have so much human-annotated data. Moreover, since these phrase embeddings are only trained to capture sentiment, they cannot be directly applied to other tasks. Our model also falls under this category, but by training our model on a large paraphrase database, we do not need additional human-annotations and the composition functions learned are not restricted to any specific tasks.

There has also been work on integrating annotation features to improve composition. For example, FCT (Yu and Dredze, 2015) uses annotation features such as POS tags and head word locations as additional features and compose word vectors with element-wise weighted average. While using such features makes sense linguistically, the assumption that phrase embeddings have to be element-wise weighted average of word embeddings is artificial. Also, the annotation features used by such methods might not be accurate due to parser errors.

Finally, our work also share similarity with neural machine translation. For example Cho et al. (2014) showed phrase embeddings can be learned with the RNN Encoder-Decoder from bilingual phrase pairs. Our model differs from their model in that our model only has the encoder part and it relates two phrases in a phrase pair with cosine similarity instead of conditional probability. We also do not only consider true paraphrase pairs but leverage negative sampling to make the model more robust. In addition, our model is trained on English paraphrases instead of bilingual phrase pairs.

5 Conclusion

In this paper, we introduced the idea of training complex compositional models for phrase embeddings on paraphrase databases. We designed a pairwise-GRU framework to encode each phrase with a GRU encoder. Compared with previous non-compositional and compositional phrase embedding methods, our framework has much better generalizability and can be re-used for any length of phrases. In addition, the experimental results on various phrase similarity tasks showed that our framework can also better capture phrase semantics and achieve state-of-the-art performances.

Acknowledgments

We would thank all the reviewers for the valuable suggestions. This project was supported by the DARPA DEFT and U.S. ARL NS-CTA. The views and conclusions contained in this document are those of the authors and should not be interpreted as representing the official policies, either expressed or implied, of the U.S. Government. The U.S. Government is authorized to reproduce and distribute reprints for Government purposes notwithstanding any copyright notation here on.

References

Colin Bannard and Chris Callison-Burch. 2005. Paraphrasing with bilingual parallel corpora. In *Proceedings of the 43rd Annual Meeting on Association for Computational Linguistics*, pages 597–604. Association for Computational Linguistics.

Danqi Chen and Christopher D Manning. 2014. A fast and accurate dependency parser using neural networks. In *Emnlp*, pages 740–750.

Kyunghyun Cho, Bart Van Merriënboer, Caglar Gulcehre, Dzmitry Bahdanau, Fethi Bougares, Holger Schwenk, and Yoshua Bengio. 2014. Learning phrase representations using rnn encoder-decoder for statistical machine translation. *arXiv preprint arXiv:1406.1078*.

Xiaocheng Feng, Lifu Huang, Duyu Tang, Bing Qin, Heng Ji, and Ting Liu. 2016. A language-independent neural network for event detection. In *The 54th Annual Meeting of the Association for Computational Linguistics*, page 66.

Juri Ganitkevitch, Benjamin Van Durme, and Chris Callison-Burch. 2013. Ppdb: The paraphrase database. In *HLT-NAACL*, pages 758–764.

Alex Graves. 2013. Generating sequences with recurrent neural networks. *arXiv preprint arXiv:1308.0850*.

Geoffrey E Hinton, Nitish Srivastava, Alex Krizhevsky, Ilya Sutskever, and Ruslan R Salakhutdinov. 2012. Improving neural networks by preventing co-adaptation of feature detectors. *arXiv preprint arXiv:1207.0580*.

Sepp Hochreiter and Jürgen Schmidhuber. 1997. Long short-term memory. *Neural computation*, 9(8):1735–1780.

Lifu Huang, Taylor Cassidy, Xiaocheng Feng, Heng Ji, Clare R Voss, Jiawei Han, and Avirup Sil. 2016. Liberal event extraction and event schema induction. In *ACL (1)*.

Nal Kalchbrenner, Edward Grefenstette, and Phil Blunsom. 2014. A convolutional neural network for modelling sentences. *arXiv preprint arXiv:1404.2188*.

Yoon Kim. 2014. Convolutional neural networks for sentence classification. *arXiv preprint arXiv:1408.5882*.

Ioannis Konstas, Srinivasan Iyer, Mark Yatskar, Yejin Choi, and Luke Zettlemoyer. 2017. Neural amr: Sequence-to-sequence models for parsing and generation. *arXiv preprint arXiv:1704.08381*.

Ioannis Korkontzelos, Torsten Zesch, Fabio Massimo Zanzotto, and Chris Biemann. 2013. Semeval-2013 task 5: Evaluating phrasal semantics. In *Second Joint Conference on Lexical and Computational Semantics (* SEM)*, volume 2, pages 39–47.

Ankit Kumar, Ozan Irsoy, Jonathan Su, James Bradbury, Robert English, Brian Pierce, Peter Ondruska, Ishaan Gulrajani, and Richard Socher. 2015. Ask me anything: Dynamic memory networks for natural language processing. *CoRR, abs/1506.07285*.

Guillaume Lample, Miguel Ballesteros, Sandeep Subramanian, Kazuya Kawakami, and Chris Dyer. 2016. Neural architectures for named entity recognition. *arXiv preprint arXiv:1603.01360*.

Tomas Mikolov, Ilya Sutskever, Kai Chen, Greg S Corrado, and Jeff Dean. 2013. Distributed representations of words and phrases and their compositionality. In *Advances in neural information processing systems*, pages 3111–3119.

Jeff Mitchell and Mirella Lapata. 2010. Composition in distributional models of semantics. *Cognitive science*, 34(8):1388–1429.

Razvan Pascanu, Tomas Mikolov, and Yoshua Bengio. 2013. On the difficulty of training recurrent neural networks. In *International Conference on Machine Learning*, pages 1310–1318.

Adam Poliak, Pushpendre Rastogi, M Patrick Martin, and Benjamin Van Durme. 2017. Efficient, compositional, order-sensitive n-gram embeddings. *EACL 2017*, page 503.

Richard Socher, Danqi Chen, Christopher D Manning, and Andrew Ng. 2013a. Reasoning with neural tensor networks for knowledge base completion. In *Advances in neural information processing systems*, pages 926–934.

Richard Socher, Brody Huval, Christopher D Manning, and Andrew Y Ng. 2012. Semantic compositionality through recursive matrix-vector spaces. In *Proceedings of the 2012 joint conference on empirical methods in natural language processing and computational natural language learning*, pages 1201–1211. Association for Computational Linguistics.

Richard Socher, Christopher D Manning, and Andrew Y Ng. 2010. Learning continuous phrase representations and syntactic parsing with recursive neural networks. In *Proceedings of the NIPS-2010 Deep Learning and Unsupervised Feature Learning Workshop*, pages 1–9.

Richard Socher, Jeffrey Pennington, Eric H Huang, Andrew Y Ng, and Christopher D Manning. 2011. Semi-supervised recursive autoencoders for predicting sentiment distributions. In *Proceedings of the conference on empirical methods in natural language processing*, pages 151–161. Association for Computational Linguistics.

Richard Socher, Alex Perelygin, Jean Y Wu, Jason Chuang, Christopher D Manning, Andrew Y Ng, Christopher Potts, et al. 2013b. Recursive deep models for semantic compositionality over a sentiment treebank. In *Proceedings of the conference on empirical methods in natural language processing (EMNLP)*, volume 1631, page 1642. Citeseer.

Kai Sheng Tai, Richard Socher, and Christopher D Manning. 2015. Improved semantic representations from tree-structured long short-term memory networks. *arXiv preprint arXiv:1503.00075*.

Stefanie Tellex, Boris Katz, Jimmy Lin, Aaron Fernandes, and Gregory Marton. 2003. Quantitative evaluation of passage retrieval algorithms for question answering. In *Proceedings of the 26th annual international ACM SIGIR conference on Research and development in informaion retrieval*, pages 41–47. ACM.

Peter D Turney. 2012. Domain and function: A dual-space model of semantic relations and compositions. *Journal of Artificial Intelligence Research*, 44:533–585.

Majid Yazdani, Meghdad Farahmand, and James Henderson. 2015. Learning semantic composition to detect non-compositionality of multiword expressions. In *EMNLP*, pages 1733–1742.

Wenpeng Yin and Hinrich Schütze. 2014. An exploration of embeddings for generalized phrases. In *ACL (Student Research Workshop)*, pages 41–47.

Mo Yu and Mark Dredze. 2015. Learning composition models for phrase embeddings. *Transactions of the Association for Computational Linguistics*, 3:227–242.

Daojian Zeng, Kang Liu, Siwei Lai, Guangyou Zhou, Jun Zhao, et al. 2014. Relation classification via convolutional deep neural network. In *COLING*, pages 2335–2344.

Jiajun Zhang, Shujie Liu, Mu Li, Ming Zhou, Chengqing Zong, et al. 2014. Bilingually-constrained phrase embeddings for machine translation. In *ACL (1)*, pages 111–121.

Jie Zhou and Wei Xu. 2015. End-to-end learning of semantic role labeling using recurrent neural networks. In *ACL (1)*, pages 1127–1137.

Author Index

Association for Computational Linguistics
209 N. Eighth Street
Stroudsburg, Pennsylvania 18360

CURRAN ASSOCIATES INC.
proceedings.com

ISBN 978-1-5108-5298-3
9 781510 852983